WIND
and
WAVES

Resting in His Promises
A 40 Day Devotional Book

Audrey Del Campo

WIND AND WAVES
RESTING IN HIS PROMISES A 40 DAY DEVOTIONAL BOOK

iUniverse books may be ordered through booksellers or by contacting:

iUniverse
1663 Liberty Drive
Bloomington, IN 47403
www.iuniverse.com
844-349-9409

ISBN: 978-1-6632-5155-8 (sc)
ISBN: 978-1-6632-5156-5 (e)

Library of Congress Control Number: 2023904526

Print information available on the last page.

iUniverse rev. date: 09/11/2023

PREFACE

Bright-eyed and bushy-tailed—ready to conquer the world. That was 4-year-old me as we moved to a new town where my dad got his first call to be a pastor right out of seminary. Little did I know, that new place I'd call home, would also be the place where my faith would be exponentially stretched and tested.

Growing up as a pastor's kid—I saw it all. The good, the bad, and the ugly of church were no strangers to me. And through it all, for some reason, I still stuck with it. Looking back, I know what "reason" it is now—God's plans and purposes for my life. When I say I've seen it all, I mean… I've seen it all. Miracles breaking through, lives being restored, hearts being set free, people plotting behind my dad's back, church committee meetings getting heated and out of control, investing in the lives of people and then watching them leave divisively. I get now why people say that faith isn't for the faint of heart. But then again… I think that's exactly what it's for on a much grander scheme. My heart, as broken and frail as it's been through life's various situations, has only been able to heal, mature and grow through my faith in Jesus. I wish I could say it was an unwavering faith—but the only unwavering thing about my story is the Presence of Jesus through it all. From the moment I was born, to where I am now, I owe it all to Him.

Jesus has helped me through crazy church dysfunction, bad relationship choices as a teenager, family struggles growing up as a pastor's kid as well as growing up with a handicapped sibling. Jesus has helped me overcome identity issues that I was held captive to by believing lies of the enemy. He walked with me on a painful journey towards healing and restoration after a divorce. Jesus saved my life from the waters of a flash flood that wanted to throw my car off of a cliff on the dirt roads of Paraguay. Jesus healed my dad and brought my family closer together after a serious health scare. Jesus healed my body when the enemy went after my blood just weeks before my pastoral ordination. I have seen the hand of God, and I have heard Him speak. He is real, He is alive, and He loves you and cares for you.

This is not a *think positive* book. This is not a *self-help* formula. This book is a collection of thoughts and Bible passages inspired by key breakthrough moments of my life that have helped my faith grow. Through the winds and waves of life's fiercest storms, God has proven to be real, true to His word, and faithfully present in my life—and it is my hope to share this truth with you. No matter what you're going through today, please believe, you can find God is in this storm.

-Audrey

DAY 1

IN THE BEGINNING, GOD CREATED MAN AND WOMAN IN His likeness—meaning, He created us to be relational. But so much deeper than that, He created us to be in a relationship with Him. Over the next forty days, you will begin to uncover the beautiful mystery of His love for you, as you draw closer to God and let Him draw close to You. I believe God wants to speak courage into your life. Speak identity. Speak security. Speak salvation. You can hear His voice as you slowly turn to Him.

Maybe you've been looking for answers for a long time but just can't seem to find them. Maybe this is your first devotional. You're reading this, and that's no coincidence. Soak in every word and wait for God to speak.

Maybe you're reading this as a last attempt to see if God is actually real and see if He speaks to you.

Maybe you feel like you're broken beyond repair. Hopeless. Lost. Like the storms of this life are just too much. The wind and waves have tossed and turned your boat for far too long. The crippling busyness that occupies our days, the political polarizations, global unrest even displayed in nature have just gotten to be too much.

If you identified with any of those things, this book is for you.

In Mark 4, the disciples were worried about everything that was going on around them. They were scared. *Terrified.* But then…Jesus. He stepped in and everything changed. That is what He does. When Jesus shows up, oftentimes, the situation itself doesn't change, though sometimes it may—but what can always happen, if we allow Him, is that He empowers us to shift our perspective. So, invite Jesus to shift your perspective today. Allow yourself to get lost in His love as you turn from focusing on the storms in your life, to the stillness and calmness of His eyes. Use this time to pour out your heart before Him, to be still and let Him love you. Don't be afraid. You are loved. You are chosen. You are redeemed. You are His.

I invite you to go to a quiet place, turn off all distractions, and just sit with Jesus. Don't worry about doing the right thing. Don't worry about saying the wrong thing. Jesus is inviting you to simply come and be with Him. Dwell. Stay. Abide. Remain.

Read: Mark 4:35-41.

Reflect: There is no storm that is out of God's control. His plans for me are good.

Pray: *Dear God, if You can calm a storm with just the sound of Your voice, help me to believe that You can and will take care of me and every one of my needs. I surrender all I am to You. Amen.*

DAY 2

LET'S START WITH A COMMON CONSENSUS THAT LIFE CAN be complicated. It's messy, it's risky, it's challenging, but in all of its chaos, there's beauty. There's beauty in knowing that God is seated above it all. He is *sovereign*. We see but a fraction of the whole picture, while God gets the main helicopter view. When you see an end, God sees a beginning. When you see chaos, God sees beauty. When you see failure, God sees opportunity.

He is the Creator of the universe, and He placed each star in the sky and knows its name. He spoke this very universe into existence with a single breath. His imagination ran wild with creativity and inspiration when He thought of you before you were in your mother's womb. You are loved by the Creator and Sustainer of the galaxies. He made *you*.

He has a plan for your life, and that plan cannot be shifted by life's happenings. God's plan cannot be threatened or challenged. Nothing happens that God doesn't already know about. Nothing catches Him by surprise. When life isn't going how you'd imagined, it's an invitation for you to stop *worrying* and start *worshiping*. It's hard, but it's worth it. Leave it all to God. He knows what He's doing.

3

Trust me, I know it can be hard to believe that He's in control when our lives seem so out of control. But this is where faith kicks in. Job shows it best. When everything he held dear was ripped away from him, what was his first instinct? To tear his robes and fall flat on his face—that sounds about right. He felt the feels...but he didn't stop there. He tore his robes and fell flat on his face, and he *worshiped*.

He tore his robes as a symbol of grief and loss. He didn't hide his emotions. He fell flat on his face because the weight of the pain was so heavy upon him that he had nothing left and could do nothing else but fall to the ground in agony. And then, He *worshiped*. He chose to give God glory in the moment of his deepest pain. Not because life was good, but because He knew that *God* was good.

It's in these moments where we need to tap into the reservoir of God's promises and believe them to be true. In the middle of the broken world we're living in, we need to trust that God is the great Healer. In the midst of so much chaos, we need to believe that God is *Shalom*— the wholeness of peace. In the folds of sorrow, we need to believe that God's joy is our strength. It's not easy, but it ends in victory because the war has already been won.

Read: Job 42:2 and Jeremiah 29:11.

Reflect: How do I respond to life's chaos?

Pray: *Dear God, You have the whole world in Your hands. Your plan is perfect and is not dependent on me. Thank You for Your goodness and faithfulness towards me. Teach me to trust You and to believe Your promises no matter what life brings. Amen.*

DAY 3

Pretend you have a glass of water. You can see perfectly through it. It's crystal clear. Now, imagine adding a little dirt to it. Now add a drop of food coloring, and maybe some grass for texture? Can you still see perfectly through it? No. Your vision has been compromised by all the stuff you've added to the water.

This happens in our lives. We were created to see Jesus, but the enemy will do anything to sabotage clarity and sends things to cloud our vision. Jesus was sent into the world to bring light to the darkness so we could see clearly. The enemy's purpose is to keep us in the darkness, so we never see the light. Sin creeps in and makes us doubt that God is good, and if we don't do anything about it, the "water" just gets murkier and murkier until we can't see God anymore. Hurt comes. Disappointment comes. Depression comes. Doubt comes. Anger comes. Unbelief comes. Social injustice comes. Sickness comes. War comes. Things come and cloud the waters. Jesus, whom we were made to see, becomes blurrier and blurrier and fades off in the distance.

The sad part is, there comes a moment where we get comfortable in the cloudy waters. We adjust our vision to be okay with the cloudy, murky, and blurry—to the point where that becomes our new normal. But there is good news! Jesus can clean the water. All we have to do is ask. We were made to have a relationship with Him, and when that relationship is compromised, we end up feeling lost, hopeless, and afraid. This is the story from the beginning—but God had a plan from the beginning: God Himself would *come down* and *dwell* with us: Jesus.

Take another look at your imagined glass of dirty water. Now, imagine taking a garden hose and just turning on the water and letting it run into the pitcher of dirty water. What's happening? *Overflow.* As the new water comes in, the old water starts flowing out. All the dirt, all the stuff that was making it cloudy, is getting washed out until all that's left is the clean water. This is what Jesus does for us. He makes it so we can see clearly. He makes us clean.

Today you're going to read about a blind beggar who was sick and tired of his life. He wanted change. He wanted to see. So, he *called out* to Jesus. Do you want change? Call out to Jesus. What's interesting about this story is that the man's miracle happens, but it happens in stages. I relate to this so much because in so many areas of my life I see God's hand, but it's a *work in progress.* God can do miracles in an instant, but He also can choose to work in stages.

This blind man slowly started to recover his sight and I think this is true for all of us. With everything we've been living through lately, having questions and blurry vision makes sense. The truth is, all of us are sitting in some sort of murky water. But Jesus wants to bring us clarity, and as His water flows, we will start to see clearly again. All you have to do is *call out* to Jesus.

Read: Mark 8:22-25 and 2 Corinthians 4:18.

Reflect: What is in my water that is making it hard for me to see Jesus? Surrender it to the Lord and ask Him to bring His perfect flow to make the waters clear again.

Pray: *Dear Jesus, thank You for being all I need to see clearly. Come and take out all the junk that is clouding my vision. Help me trust in Your timing and persevere through the process. Amen.*

DAY 4

WE ALL FIGHT SO MANY DIFFERENT BATTLES IN LIFE. Battles are chaotic and scary, and they can be incredibly overwhelming joy-stealers. It is particularly easy to listen to all the voices that surround us in these moments of battle. So many things are fighting for our attention. So many voices speak into our lives every day. They can be voices of discouragement, defeat, destruction, or disbelief. They can be voices of encouragement, victory, and life. It's our choice to decide which voices we are going to listen to.

Many times, the voices in my own head are guided by what I *see* and not guided by *faith*. For example, I can get extremely anxious when I can't see the next step or when I'm clouded by uncertainty. The voice of anxiety tells me to worry. It tries to convince me that God is not in control. It tells me that I am not going to be okay. In those moments, it is crucial to remember the promises and truth of His Word and to remind myself that God has called me to be strong and courageous—to trust Him no matter what my eyes see.

Battles come and go, but God's faithfulness endures forever. That is my security; that is where my identity lies.

I am more than a conqueror. I am victorious. I am on the winning team. The battle has already been won.

How would our perspective on hardships change if we looked at them through Christ's lens? Even in the face of a vast army, even when we feel like we're battling against something we don't have a chance against—that's when we need to activate God's promises. It is imperative in those moments to *faith it 'til you make it*. No matter what we battle in life, the battle is the Lord's, and we can rest in knowing that our God has never lost a battle, and He's not going to start now.

So, we *stand*. We *fight*—not in our own strength, but in the strength of the Lord who never fails. We *worship*—whether things are going well or not. We *worship* because God is good, and He never changes. We *surrender*. We let go of the plan in our heads. We let go of our own battle strategy and put our weapons down. Instead, we *bow down, worship,* and *watch* God's victory unfold.

Read: 2 Chronicles 32:7-8.

Reflect: What battles am I facing in life right now that are weighing me down? With God on my side, there is no battle I can't overcome. He is fighting for me. Be still, rest in Him, and watch His deliverance unfold.

Pray: *Dear God, it is such a weight off my shoulders knowing that You will fight my battles. Teach me to trust and to be still in You. Amen.*

DAY 5

WHEN WE TRUST GOD WITH OUR STRUGGLES, HE challenges and changes our perspective. To be honest, I think many times we don't talk to God or others about our struggles because we don't want to be held accountable. But something shifts, not only in our perspective, but within our very core, when we bring God into the arena.

God challenged a prophet named Ezekiel thousands of years ago. He brought Ezekiel to a valley that was covered with old, dry, dead bones. Then God asked him a very interesting question: "Can these bones live?" Honestly, I would have said, "No shot." However, Ezekiel knew very well the ways of God, and he answered, "Sovereign LORD, only you know" (Ezekiel 37:3, NIV). That answer blows me away because Ezekiel wasn't *denying* the reality of the very dry and very dead bones, but he *chose* to acknowledge the greatness and power of God, in spite of what he saw.

Ezekiel saw dry bones, but God told him to speak life over them. That seems pretty pointless. A little illogical. But he obeyed. Ezekiel stood over that valley, and instead of relying on what he saw, he opened his mouth and started prophesying the words of life that God told him to speak. As soon as the words left his mouth, the ground began to shake, and the bones started to rattle, rise, and come together, bone to bone! Then they were given the breath of life.

When you are facing an impossible situation but start speaking words of *life* and trusting in God, something *will* happen. It may not happen immediately. It probably won't happen the way you want it to happen or think it should happen. But something *has* to happen because when you speak the word of the Lord, it does not go unnoticed in the spiritual realm. The transformation of those dry bones was a message of hope for the spiritually dead nation of Israel then, and it is a message of hope for the spiritually dead things around us now.

Don't give up if you don't see changes right away. Keep praying for God to bring a cure for diseases. Pray for God to heal the racism in our country and all over the world. Pray for your family members and friends who don't know Jesus. Pray for your heart. Keep speaking life. Keep believing because God is working. One of my favorite worship songs, "Way Maker," by Sinach, says: *"Even when I don't see it, you're working. Even when I can't feel it, you're working. You never stop, you never stop working."*

Stand over your dark valley today. Maybe all you see is death—no chance of life … no chance of anything. Stand up. Be bold and speak God's words of life. Don't give up. You may see a valley of dry bones, but God will transform them into bones that are alive with promise and hope. When you begin to speak over your circumstances, ask God to align your heart with His, so that *His* will is done, not yours. And never forget, this isn't power of positivity. This is the move of the Holy Spirit empowering you to live by faith and not by sight. This is Jesus.

Read: Ezekiel 37:1-14.

Reflect: What is my valley of dry bones? What is God asking me to speak? What do I see? What is God asking me to believe?

Pray: *Dear Lord, help me see what you see. I see a whole lot of nothing sometimes, but help me to see beyond that, to speak life to dry bones and believe in the impossible. If You're guiding me, I will speak, and I will believe. Amen.*

DAY 6

WHEN YOU FEEL ATTACKED, WHAT IS YOUR INSTINCT?

We are all wired with a tendency to either fight back or run away. Fight or flight. Today I want you to really think about the way you respond in the face of difficulties. Running away is an option, and it usually involves things like denial, anger, bitterness, hurt, fear, anxiety, and resentment. Fighting can result in these same emotions if we choose to fight our own way. But when we know that God is fighting for us and with us, our focus shifts from the giant to the Giant Slayer.

Consider the familiar story of little David and the big, tall Goliath. While every man in Israel's army was afraid of the Philistines, and especially Goliath, David was brave enough to say, "This is *not* okay. If no one is going to fight this giant, I *will* because I *know* who's on my side." And David was able to kill that giant with a slingshot and five smooth stones that hit their mark.

How long have you been hurting? How long has that giant been looking down on you, threatening you, and making you run in fear? Too long. It's time to get up, look that giant straight in the eye, and remind it that God has already won.

Whatever you're going through right now, this is your *training ground*. Be bold enough to trust that God can use your time in the dry desert to help shift your focus back on Him. God is equipping you and preparing you with strategies and tools to be able to go out and conquer those giants. In your current training ground, God is building your perseverance, your hope, your trust, your obedience, and your dependency on Him. And when the time is right, you'll be able to step in front of that giant and defeat it, in God's strength.

Choosing to stand up against a giant isn't guaranteed to make you popular. The soldiers mocked David, who was just a little shepherd boy, and even David's brother spoke against him. King Saul clothed David in all his royal armor trying to equip him his own way. But David was confident in the Lord and what he learned in his training ground. He knew he would see the enemy of Israel defeated. God isn't looking for superhumans. He's not looking for the overtly talented or most obvious choice. He's looking for anyone who's willing to be *obedient*. With a stone and a slingshot and a heart full of confidence in the Lord, David defeated the giant. Because of Jesus' victory on the cross, you can too.

David could have easily looked back on his life and been full of resentment—how his brothers got all the attention, and he was left out back in the pasture with all the sheep. But it's in that pasture where he learned everything that would be key in his rise to victory. Don't underestimate your story—don't despise your past. In God, there is no wasted time. No season is unimportant. He uses all things for His glory.

Read: 1 Samuel 17.

Reflect: What giants have been keeping me in fear? Am I willing to truly believe that God is bigger than any giant I might face?

Pray: *Dear Jesus, today I give You my fear. Fill me with Your truth, and shut my ears to all the lies. Help me to stand up fully confident in knowing that You still slay giants today. Fix my eyes on you. Amen.*

DAY 7

LIFE CAN BE CRAZY. ADD A LITTLE UNCERTAINTY, A PINCH of doubt, a touch of fear, and voilà! Before we know it, we lose sight of Christ in the midst of it all. The enemy—the devil, Satan, the accuser—will make sure that all we can see is his concoction of pure chaos. In doing this, he makes us doubt the goodness of God—and when we doubt His goodness, it's a downward spiral from there. Prepare yourself for a holy truth bomb...

In John 16:33, Jesus tells his disciples the way it is. No sugarcoating anything. You *will* have trouble, He said.

When we choose to follow Christ, a magic portal does not open. We do not get to walk through a door into a rose-tinted perfect world. No, we will have troubles. We will go through pain. There will be persecution. We will go through moments of uncertainty and despair.

These are things that come with the world because it is a broken world. But because Jesus overcame death on the cross, He overcame the world and is seated at the right hand of the Father with full authority. That same power that raised Christ from the grave is living in us, too. A life with Jesus isn't a life without trouble; it's a life of faith, security, and confidence that He is walking with us *through* the trouble. It's that blessed assurance that the battle has been won because Jesus did not stay in the tomb. We are on the winning side! Jesus came so that we could live an abundant life. But don't confuse *abundant* with *easy*. Abundance is knowing that in Jesus we have all we need for every moment of our life.

So, *fear not*. There are about 365 instances in the Bible where this phrase is used. One for every day of the year. God knew we would need this kind of reassurance because our hearts are so frail. We are so weak on our own. Fear paralyzes us. And when we are paralyzed, darkness has a chance to advance and invade our thoughts.

So here is the challenge: choose faith over fear today and every day after. Don't follow the saying, "fake it till you make it." Instead try what was mentioned in day 4, "*faith* it till you make it." Walking in faith doesn't mean *never* being afraid. We can still feel afraid, but we can also take steps forward in faith. Walking in faith doesn't mean we deny reality, we just embrace it with a different hope. We shift our focus from relying on ourselves to totally depending on Christ. Don't get stuck in fear. Look beyond the fear. *Surrender. Trust. Obey. Repeat.*

Read: John 10:10 and John 16:33.

Reflect: I lay down all my fears and anxieties before You, Lord. You have overcome. Help me see how a truly abundant life only comes from You.

Pray: *Dear Jesus, thank You that You overcame the world! Your victory is my victory. Your triumph is my triumph. Because You overcame, I will overcome. Thank You for that promise. Help me rest in You, knowing that You've got me. Amen.*

DAY 8

THERE WAS A MOMENT IN MY LIFE WHERE I HONESTLY thought that I would never be able to tell others about Jesus ever again because of the brokenness of my story. The accusatory voices, the stares of judgment without walking a mile in my shoes got very real. So real, that I decided to give up. After my dad had convinced me to re-apply for seminary, I withdrew my application. Shortly after, I got a phone call from a lovely young lady from the Gordon-Conwell Theological Seminary Admissions Office asking if I was okay. No one had asked me that in a long time. I was not okay. Before I knew it, I was letting it all out. She listened. She heard my story—the brokenness and all—and said, "I'm so sorry for those lies you've believed. Let me tell you some truths: you are God's daughter. You are loved. You are called for such a time as this, and your story doesn't disqualify you, it makes you even more qualified to be able to speak restoration to the broken. Now, shall I reinstitute your application?" The rest is history.

The woman in Mark 5 was suffering from a serious blood related illness for 12 years. This made her ceremonially unclean—that meant that she couldn't by law touch anyone or be near anyone because that would "contaminate" others. Can you imagine that? 12 years of isolation. 12 years of being rejected and marginalized by something that was out of her control. She spent everything she had trying to find a cure—until she heard Jesus was in town.

I felt like this woman—so much shame and confusion. But Jesus healed me, as He healed her. I wish I could say that my faith was as strong as hers as she defied all odds and reached out to touch him among the multitude. I wasn't that bold. I was still believing that maybe I should be isolated. But God brought a woman into my life who pulled me out, grabbed my hand, and helped bring me to Jesus. She brought me one step closer to my healing and restoration, and for that I am forever grateful.

One touch, and this woman was healed instantly from her bleeding. In one second, the trajectory of her life was forever changed. Unclean to *healed*. Marginalized to *accepted*. Outcast to *daughter*. All in one encounter with Jesus—because that's all it takes. So, what are you waiting for? Get up. Run to Jesus. He's waiting, arms wide open. In this story, He was walking in one direction, and the woman was chasing after Him. In the here and now— He's not walking away from you, but towards you. Will you meet Him? Every step you take is one step closer. Are people talking about you behind your back as you make your way to Him? Probably. Will they stop once you've made it? Probably not. But people will come and go, opinions will rise and fade—Jesus will always stay, and your healing and wholeness are worth the stirring of the pot as long as you make it to Jesus.

Read: Mark 5:25-34.

Reflect: What are things that are keeping me on the wayside from running towards Jesus? Do I believe that all it takes is one touch for my life to be changed?

Pray: *Dear God, teach me to rest in You and have faith that You are with me. Nothing is impossible for You. You look at me and call me, "Daughter," "Son," and have a life of freedom and healing in Your plans for me. Amen.*

DAY 9

One of the hardest things in life is waiting. And waiting is so incredibly difficult because of our desperate need to want things to happen *now*. Unfortunately, this isn't how things in the kingdom work out. Waiting, perseverance, and growing in the process is a huge part of what grows our faith.

God has used the story of Abraham over and over again to speak life into me and remind me that His promises always come true, even when it seems like the time of waiting will never end. Abraham was 75 years old when God told him that he would be a father of nations…75 and not even one child. Yet, Abraham held on to this promise and followed God. He did not see the promise come to life until 25 years later. That's right… he was 100 years old when the son of the promise, Isaac, was born! Can you imagine the questions among those 25 years of waiting? The feeling that maybe God forgot. That maybe you misunderstood what God said. That maybe the promise was meant for someone else. Or even doing what his wife Sarah did and sneak in a little strategy of your own to help God a little to expedite the process.

I've been there. I remember asking God if He forgot about my family when my youngest sister was born.

She was born three months early and weighed in at one pound six oz. A few months later, her retinas detached and she became blind. A few years later, she developed epilepsy. Shortly after, she was diagnosed with cerebral palsy. Shortly after that, we were told she'd never walk, talk or be able to feed herself or go to the bathroom on her own. The whole time we were praying as a church for healing over my sister. Word from the Lord came and said, "I have a plan for her." That filled me with so much hope. I figured it would be soon that God would heal her, and it would spark revival in central Jersey. But the miracle never came. Actually, the more we prayed, the worse things got. It didn't make sense. Soon after that I started questioning God. *What did you mean? Are you going to heal her? I don't understand.*

20 years later, there's still been no healing like the one I'd imagined, but God was right… He did have a plan for her, and my family. For Abraham, He got his son which eventually would become everything God said—a whole nation, Israel. For my family, things were a little different—but in the waiting I did learn something very valuable: God's promises in Jesus are yes and amen. Yes, and amen doesn't mean that things are going to come out the way I want or envision them. Yes, and amen means that God is God, and God is good and what He said He will accomplish. Did He have a plan for my sister? Yes. He used her life to teach my family a deeper love, deeper mercy and deeper compassion that made us stronger on all fronts. Through Britney, my sweet sister, God taught us that the most important lessons are learned in the waiting.

Read: Genesis 21:1-7.

Reflect: What events in my life have caused me to stop believing in God's promises? *Pause.* Bring them to God and ask Him to awaken my faith once more.

Pray: *Dear Jesus, thank You for Your faithful love. Thank you for being a God of promises, and for fulfilling them in Your time. Help me to keep believing, especially when it feels like nothing is happening. Amen.*

DAY 10

OUR GOD IS A GOD OF HOPE. NO MATTER WHAT YOU HAVE gone through in life—whether the difficult situations were self-inflicted or happenstance—there is hope. Jesus keeps hope alive because He *is* alive. In my own life, I look back and what I see now is a landscape of hills and valleys that when I look closely, all helped to position me where I am now. Things could have ended up very differently had I chosen to process everything differently... but God never let me go, and I am beyond grateful for His Sovereign hand and providence on my life. I bet if you look back, and invite God to show you, you'll see His Sovereign hand and providence over your life—yes. Even in those dark, hopeless, joyless valleys where it's hard to believe that He's actually there with you.

This image of hills and valleys is really what life is. It is not a straight-lined journey from Point A to Point B. It is much more complex than that. This really annoys me because I like having a plan, and when things start getting in the way that mess with the plan, I get frustrated. A lot of the things in my life that have caused heartache and heartbreak have been my insistence on holding on to *my* plan and not looking up towards what was ahead. Many things in life we may not see coming, but God gives us all we need to confront whatever may come. One of the greatest passages in scripture that has spoken hope over me in times of scaling hills I didn't see coming is Psalm 121, *"I lift up my eyes to the hills, where does my help come from? My help comes from the Lord, the Maker of heaven and earth."*

There is so much comfort in just that opening verse. We get so caught up in looking *around*, that we forget to look *up*. Our hope is not found in the circumstantial, but the celestial—in Christ alone. Only looking up will I be able to find my true source of help. Who but the Creator and Sustainer of the universe can help me scale the craziest of hills? Who but the One who does not sleep, or rest can help me traverse the darkest of valleys? Who but the One whose breath lives inside my lungs can help me get to my destination? Only Him. Christ alone.

This Psalm is known as a *song of ascent*—a song that the Israelites would sing on their journey towards Jerusalem for their festivals. The terrain was rough—the roads were scary, but they had these songs they would sing to shift their perspective so they could be reminded of what they were going towards at the end of their journey. No matter the hills and valleys that you may scale, know that God is with you. He is your help, and He is your destination.

Read: Psalm 121.

Reflect: How have I handled the hills and valleys in my life? Do I go to God for help, or do I try to scale my own way?

Pray: *Father, Creator of the universe, I ask that You open my heart so that I might trust You in every season of my life—especially while traversing the hills and valleys. Amen.*

DAY 11

ONE OF THE EARLIEST MEMORIES I HAVE AS A CHILD WAS stumbling upon a meeting I was not supposed to see. A couple of church leaders had my dad cornered in a room telling him things like, "You will never be our pastor," "We will make sure you and your family leave." As a five-year-old, that was very damaging to hear. Something shifted in me. I decided in that moment that it was my responsibility to hold my family together and to give absolutely no one a reason to kick my family out. So, I did everything I could to "out serve" everyone. I became a top-notch people-pleaser. I was the first one to show up to have everything set up, and the last one to leave to make sure everything was cleaned up. Outwardly I smiled to show that everything was okay, while inside I was dying a slow death trying to figure out how people could be so mean and then lift up their hands in worship at church. It wasn't until later as an adult, through counseling, that I realized that this persona was created in order to protect my heart, even though it was actually breaking. It wasn't until I learned to forgive and let go, that I was actually set free.

Childhood and early teenage years are so formational. Trauma that we experience back then can take a toll on our spiritual and emotional health as adults which play a part on all fronts of our relational lives. So, here's where the key lies—we cannot change what happened in the past, but we can invite Jesus to bring healing *now*, to change the course of our future and find true joy in the journey.

Life as we know will not always go as planned. Loved ones die. Marriages end. Friends turn away. Sickness strikes. You feel hurt. You experience pain. You have moments where you think you can't do life anymore. Maybe you're in that place right now, and you're asking God if there's any way out. There is. Jesus is the way. The God of hope wants to fill you with all joy, regardless of your circumstances. This kind of joy has *nothing* to do with what's happening in your life and *everything* to do with *who* God is. This kind of joy allows you to look at a tough situation and say, "Yet I will rejoice in the Lord, I will be joyful in God my Savior" (Habakkuk 3:18, NIV).

That's right, *joy.* What is joy? What does it mean to be joyful? Well, you might say a synonym for joy is happiness, but they are actually different. Happiness is rooted in momentary pleasure. Joy is rooted in something eternal… in *Someone,* in God. When we realize *who* God is and *who we are* in Christ, we learn that our joy doesn't depend on our circumstances; it depends on who God is, and He is good. This might be really hard to digest especially if you feel like God hasn't been good to you. But as you've read, life isn't always going to bring what we may consider "happily ever after's" along the journey. Even the greatest heroes of the Bible experienced sorrow on their way to victory. The greatest lesson we can learn in our lifetime is knowing that God is with us, and if

He is with us, we can experience a greater joy than this world can offer.

Read: Habakkuk 3:17-19 and Nehemiah 8:10.

Reflect: How can I change my mindset to activate God's joy in my life?

Pray: *Dear God, help me to find joy no matter what's happening in my life. Help me to see Your hand at work and to trust in You. Help me to always believe that the joy of the Lord is my strength. Amen.*

DAY 12

"It's easy to follow when the path is clear. But when the path bends towards uncertainty I'm filled with fear … but I will carry on. I will stay my course. I don't know where You're leading me, but I know I can trust that Your plans are good, that You're guiding my steps, and when all hope seems lost, I will trust even then in Your faithfulness."

Those are the words to a song I wrote called "Pressing On." I wrote it in 2018 while serving as a leader at a youth camp. I fell asleep praying about my struggling marriage, and I woke up early the following morning with both the lyrics and the melody in my head. In the middle of my unknown, my questions and my doubts, God came and reminded my heart that it's okay to feel the way I did, but it's not okay to stay there. *Don't get stuck in the doubt; move in faith.*

I could picture Abraham singing these words to God on his way up the mountain after God asked him to sacrifice his one and only son, Isaac. After waiting 25 years for God to give him a son, now came this crazy request. But Abraham *obeyed*. God didn't tell him where he was going. He just told Abraham to walk, and He'd let him know when he arrived. This wasn't new for Abraham as this is exactly how his journey with God began when he was 75 years old. Through Abraham's life, we see a man whose faith was forged through the waiting and trusting in God.

Just as Abraham was about to sacrifice his son, God intervened and provided a ram for the sacrifice instead. This is the most beautiful foreshadowing of what Jesus would come to do for us: take our place on the altar to be slain for our sin. *Jesus took our place.* That is God's merciful provision for us. He is *Jehovah Jireh*, God our Provider.

Have you started walking a path of faith but then grew frightened and lost your way? You might feel like you're walking with a broken compass and north keeps shifting. When we give God the compass and follow His love, which is our true north, He will show us where we need to go. So, carry on. Stay the course. You can trust that His plans for you are good, and when you just can't see the path ahead, rest in His faithfulness. He will come through, just as He did for Abraham and Isaac. Just as Jesus did for humanity. You may not see the purpose as you're scaling the mountain, but on the mountaintop, God will reveal what you could not see on the journey up.

Read: Genesis 22:1-19.

Reflect: What path am I on right now? Do I need to exchange my broken compass for Christ's true north?

Pray: *Holy Spirit, thank You for guiding me when I don't know what to do, what to say, or where to go. Tune my heart to hear Your voice. Guide my heart to follow Your true north. Teach me to trust You even when I can't see or understand. Amen.*

DAY 13

Sometimes God brings us to the desert to create a thirst for Him in us. It's so easy to get caught up in life's demands—school, work, family, friends, church—and forget that we *need* God. We forget that He has to sit on the throne of our hearts in order for us to live a life of abundance. It's so easy to give up His place in our hearts and let other things sneak their way into the throne room. That's when things start to fall apart.

This isn't to say that every bad moment in our lives is God's way of getting our attention. No. Our God is a good Father. However, sometimes it takes hitting rock bottom to look up. Many times, God *allows* situations to happen, but He's there. The most important thing to remember is this: it's not about the desert. It's about our God who gives us a way through it.

What gets us through the desert? Hope. Hope in God. Trusting in Jesus. Activating the power of the Holy Spirit in our lives. What gets us through the desert? Worship. Worship changes everything because it is actively choosing God over circumstances. It is actively putting God back on the throne, and when He's on the throne, our perspective shifts.

In our lives, we are all going to go through deserts. Maybe it's your marriage, or a relationship with a family member, friend, or coworker. Maybe it's an addiction you can't seem to break. Maybe it's a loved one's sickness or death. Maybe it's your situation at school. Maybe it's your job. Maybe it's your self-image. No matter what desert you may find yourself in, God is there. He's with you. Choose worship. In the desert, He still speaks. He's still God. He's still good. And through it all, we can know that because God is in the equation, nothing is wasted. He can work all things for good.

Just like for the Israelites, after a time away in exile, God promised to bring them back home rejoicing. He promised that there would be a day where the past would no longer need to be remembered, because all that would matter would be all the *new* that was in the making. Don't fear the desert, worship and trust God on your way through.

Read: Isaiah 43:18-19 and Hosea 2:14-15.

Reflect: God's got me.

Pray: *Dear Jesus, help me remember that You are in control of everything. You're holding me. You love me. Strengthen my faith through each desert I face as I learn to trust You and build my hope on You. Amen.*

DAY 14

By now, you've heard of God the Father, Creator of the universe. You've heard of His Son—Jesus, who was sent into the world to reconcile us with God the Father because sin kept us apart. Jesus came in obedience, and once His mission on earth was fulfilled, He went back to His Father in heaven. But there's one more person left—the Holy Spirit. Jesus' very essence sent to us to comfort, guide and walk with us until Jesus comes again.

Let's time travel for a second. You're one of Jesus' twelve disciples—one of His closest friends, and Jesus says He's *leaving*. What kind of thoughts would be going through your mind? You gave up everything you had to follow this man. You ate, slept, walked, and did ministry with Him for three years … and now He says He's leaving. Can you imagine the fear? The loneliness? The questions?

Jesus knows what you're feeling, so He looks at you and says, "If you love me, keep my commands. And I will ask the Father, and he will give you another advocate to help you and be with you forever—the Spirit of truth. The world cannot accept Him, because it neither sees Him nor knows Him. But you know Him, for He lives with you and will be in you" (John 14:16-17, NIV). To this day that promise stands true. You are not alone. If you have given your life to Jesus, then you have the Holy Spirit inside of you to guide you to all truth.

So, don't be afraid. If you are feeling far from the Lord, don't go any farther away. You can draw near to God because He has already drawn near to you. I love thinking of Him as a waterfall. The water just keeps coming and coming. It doesn't stop or ever run dry. He doesn't change. *I* choose whether *I* want to stay under the flow or walk away. He's constant.

Draw close, right here, right now. He is for you. He is with You. He loves you. You are not an orphan. You have everything you need inside you: Jesus, through the power of the Holy Spirit, to the praise of God the Father. Believe God's promises. Call on the Holy Spirit and live life not just going through the motions, but empowered and purposeful. He gives you everything you need for every second of every day. That is who He is and will forever be.

This brought me so much comfort in serious moments of loneliness. I could be surrounded by hundreds of people, yet still feel so alone. But when I understood the power of the Holy Spirit and what He does within me, it changed my life. I went from being a victim to becoming empowered and believing what He said of me.

Read: John 14.

Reflect: I am not alone. I have the very essence of Jesus living in me through the Holy Spirit.

Pray: *Dear God, thank You for such an amazing promise! I know that I am not alone. You are with me always. Teach me to become more aware of the Holy Spirit in my life. Amen.*

DAY 15

IMAGINE A DAD PLAYING WITH HIS LITTLE GIRL. SHE IS UP on a ledge and her dad holds out his arms and yells, "Jump! I'll catch you!" And without thinking twice, she goes for it! Like that loving dad, God is standing right in front of you and telling you to jump into His arms. He knows life has been tough. He knows people have let you down. He knows that you've been hurt or are hurting. He gets why you'd be hesitant to just jump. But He's asking you to do so anyway. Are you brave enough to try?

Take it from me, there's no better place to be than in God's arms. I've tried jumping into other people's "*arms*" trying to find comfort and solutions to no avail. Temporary effects, but nothing lasting. Jesus has been the only One who has actually changed my life and brought true healing. And it's not that I'm perfect now and have it all together—no. Every morning it's about waking up and standing on the ledge and making the decision all over again. Will I choose to trust God and jump into His arms today or trust myself and what I want to do?

My advice—jump. Just do it. Surrender all your fears. All your past mistakes. All your disappointments. As cliché as it sounds, *let go and let God*. He won't judge.

He won't disappoint. He won't reject. He'll just hold you. Heal you. Love you.

The story today is about a woman who had a very questionable past. She didn't deserve to even be close to Jesus. As a matter of fact, because of all that she had done, and being a woman in that time period, it was basically illegal to come near a teacher like Jesus. But she took her chances, and with a surrendered heart, she went to His feet. She didn't care what others thought at that point; she just knew where she needed to be. She dared to jump.

This seems daunting because we are wired to worry about ourselves and our safety. We are all about self-preservation, but God is asking us to trust Him to preserve our lives. There comes a time where you just need to stop protecting yourself and let God care for you. You might not feel worthy to let God care for you. You might not feel like you have anything to offer, but all He's looking for is a willing heart. A surrendered heart. A heart willing to break the mold and give it all to Him. Can you give Jesus your whole heart today?

Read: Luke 7:36-50.

Reflect: This woman had nothing left. She gave what she had and surrendered at Jesus' feet. Everyone else thought she was dirty. Jesus thought she was worthy. So am I.

Pray: *Dear God, thank You for accepting me just as I am. I'm scared, but I want to jump into Your arms. Help me to trust You. You won't let me fall. You won't let me go. Thank you. Amen.*

DAY 16

YOU'RE PROBABLY FAMILIAR WITH PSALM 23: *"THE LORD is my shepherd, I shall not want."* We repeat it and quote it— we hear it at funerals, and it makes us feel better. But as easily as we throw it around, we can easily forget just how deep the promise is. I know I tend to forget, especially when I'm caught in that "valley of the shadow of death." So, let's take a look at it together, piece by piece.

The Lord is my shepherd. He is in control. I am a sheep. I must learn to know His voice. His voice leads me where to go. He will take care of me.

I shall not want. God supplies and satisfies everything I could ever need. *He* is all I need.

He makes me lie down in green pastures. He is my rest. He is my *shalom,* my peace. When everything around me is dry and barren, He leads me to a place of abundance.

He leads me beside quiet waters. He is my purification. He is my refreshment. He leads me to the well because He *is* the well. In the uproar of the wind and waves, He is my stillness.

He refreshes my soul. He is my healing. He lifts me up. He binds my wounds. He fills me.

He guides me along the right path for His name's sake. He corrects my path as I learn to trust Him and let Him lead.

The right path might not always look the way I think it should, but if He is guiding, it will be for His glory. I will be okay.

Even though I walk through the darkest valley, I will fear no evil, for You are with me. He is my protector. He is my deliverer. He is my comforter. He is my salvation. He never leaves me. He is still leading, even along the dark and frightening roads—"the valley of the shadow of death," as the KJV says.

Your rod and Your staff, they comfort me. His guidance and counsel bring me life if I let Him guide my path. He pulls me back in when I wander. He loves me enough to correct me, and in the end, my soul is comforted because He keeps me safe.

You prepare a table before me in the presence of my enemies. He honors those who honor Him. If God is for me, nothing can stand against me. He is always working things for my good.

You anoint my head with oil; my cup overflows. He chooses me. He wants to fill me. He wants to use me.

Surely Your goodness and mercy will follow me all the days of my life. He is with me wherever I go. His mercies are new every morning. His blessings follow me when I choose to follow Him.

And I will dwell in the house of the LORD forever. This is the promise! When my time on this earth is over, I am going home to live with Him forever! Death on this side of eternity is not the end, it marks the beginning of life eternal.

Read: Psalm 23.

Reflect: If I have God, I have all that I need.

Pray: *Dear God, thank You for Your promises. Thank You for the assurance that even though trouble may come, if You are leading me, I will be okay. Restoration and still waters are a part of Your plan for my life, as are the dark valleys. You walk with me through it all. Thank You. Amen.*

DAY 17

Who am I? This was a question that has kept me up at night for many years. Foundationally, I knew I was loved by God and my family, yet I felt the need to continue to validate it. This became the root for bad decisions that left my soul hurting. I was lacking a sense of true *identity*. I believe that just as I struggled with it as a teenager and into my early 20's, many people are struggling with it now which is causing a lot of dark nights of the soul.

Our deepest identity is found in Christ. You are His child. You were created for Him. Before the foundation of the Earth, you were on His mind. You are His masterpiece, His workmanship, His handiwork. The Greek word for "handiwork" is *poiema,* or "poem." You are God's poem. He was inspired when He thought of you. My mom always says, "You are God's poem, inspiration of His heart."

You are loved. You matter. He formed you with such care, such tenderness. He created you perfectly, in His image. And most importantly, God is not finished with you yet. He loves you just the way you are but loves you too much to leave you the way you are. When we allow Him, He works in and through our circumstances to mold and shape us into His image.

However, when we let difficult circumstances get the best of us, we might feel that God has abandoned us. But even when we feel like we are forgotten, worthless, or stuck, God is with us and is refining us. Part of the refining process is going through fire. Fire is warm, but fire burns. The heat can be comforting or terrifying, and it's easy to forget that if God is in control, we will not burn. A potter's jar must go into the fiery kiln to be glazed. A piece of silver must go through the fire to be purified. Each piece of art must be removed from the fire at just the right moment. Too soon, and the piece is unfinished. Too long, and it is ruined.

God is the perfect potter, the perfect silversmith. He loves you too much to take you out of the fire too soon; He loves you too much to leave you in there for too long. Believe in the power you have to press on because of the Holy Spirit living in you. Believe that you can find peace and joy no matter what situation comes your way because Jesus walks with you. His love for you is so real, so faithful, and so relentless. The enemy *will* come and try to steal your joy and rob you of your peace. It's what he does. But partnered with Christ, you are in full control—the enemy can't take away that which you refuse to give up. Peace and joy are yours through Christ, and your identity lies in Him. God will be faithful to complete what He started in you.

Read: Ephesians 2:10 and Philippians 1:6.

Reflect: How does it feel to be God's inspiration?

Pray: *Dear Heavenly Father, I am Your child! Help me see myself the way You see me. Help me to believe that I am everything You say I am. Help me to trust You, even in the fire. Amen.*

DAY 18

When I became Assistant Pastor at my new church in New Providence, NJ, I began doing morning prayer walks around the town. This helped me to get the lay of the land, my steps in, and it set my mind on Christ every morning before diving into the day's work. One morning God taught me a powerful lesson about perseverance and endurance.

On this particular morning, I felt God say, *no music today. Just me and you. No distractions.* So, I listened, and began my walk. Without the music, I realized how keenly aware I was of my surroundings—I was becoming increasingly aware of the fact that I kept getting pebbles in my sneakers as I walked. Now, me being me, I tried to ignore the pebbles and kept walking because I had a plan. I had to beat my time and distance from the day before—so, naturally, there was no room for stopping or taking a break.

Then God was like: *"You've got perseverance and endurance all wrong, kid. What good is it to walk with pebbles in your shoes? You're not comfortable and eventually it'll make you start walking funny and throw off your form and that can lead to injury. Not only will you not make it to the finish line if you're injured, but you can't help anyone along the way. Also, you're thinking more about the pebbles than talking to Me. They're distracting you. Perseverance and endurance are not about not stopping for the purpose of pressing on. They're about having the discernment of knowing when to stop in order to keep pressing on. This is what I meant when I said, "throw off everything that hinders and so easily entangles you." Sure, sometimes you can do it mid journey where you don't need to stop. But sometimes, when there are lots of pebbles in your shoes, you HAVE to stop and it's okay."*

Then, I looked up and saw a huge rock at the end of this dead-end street and God was like, *"I'm the Rock you're grounded on, so have a seat and take out those pebbles so we can keep walking and talking."*

Friends, for too long we have tried to ignore the pebbles. It's okay to stop. What's not okay is to stay stopped. Also, we are surrounded by a great cloud of witnesses who will encourage us along the journey. Imagine a stadium full of people cheering you on your race. It's real! All of heaven is cheering you on, too.

When the lies you are hearing are getting louder than the truth (pebbles start filling your shoes), surround yourself with people who will remind you of the truth. When things weigh you down, throw them off through prayer and the power of the Holy Spirit. When you start to feel discouraged, check in with someone who will encourage you and keep you accountable. When you start to feel like you can't do it, remember Jesus. He walked every step towards the cross, even as people were spitting on Him, hitting Him, whipping Him, placing the crown of thorns on His head, and nailing Him to the cross. He endured all this because He had His eyes on the prize—you.

Read: Hebrews 12:1-3.

Reflect: Who in my circle of family and friends can speak the truth to me when I feel like giving up? Who will help me refocus my eyes on Jesus and help me discern when I need to stop and shake the pebbles out of my shoes?

Pray: *Dear Jesus, thank You for reminding me that all I need is You. Thank You for running Your race for me. Now help me run my race for You. Amen.*

DAY 19

We go through life trying to figure out where we belong, where we fit in. We search to see who really loves us, and we try to find things to fill our lives so we feel full and satisfied. The simple truth is, you can search every nook and cranny of this universe to find things to fill you, but the only thing that can truly satisfy you, fill you, and make you feel complete and whole is God and His love.

When you encounter God's love for real—not just an emotional high—you step into a new identity. You realize who you are in Christ. You realize that you have been *redeemed.* To redeem means to gain something back in return for payment. You have been bought back by the blood of Jesus. That's crazy amazing! Now there is nothing that can separate you from God's love!

The apostle Paul gets excited about this in Romans 8:38-39 (NIV): "Neither death nor life, neither angels nor demons, neither the present nor the future, nor any powers, neither height nor depth, nor anything else in all creation, will be able to separate us from the love of God that is in Christ Jesus our Lord." This is an incredible promise. The Father saw that we needed a Savior, so He sent His Son, Jesus. The Son obediently came and became like one of us and walked in this world to build relationships with those around Him, to bring them close to the Father. His mission was to die, because He was the only one who could, so that we could be reconciled with the Father. Redeemed! His blood has made you His own. His blood has set you free.

In this Bible story, a woman deserved to die for what she did wrong. But Jesus did not accuse her. He forgave her, then challenged her to get up and go and sin no more. There is a divine exchange that can never be matched: shame for mercy. I give Him my shame, and He gives me His mercy. I give Him my wrongs, and He makes me right before the Father. I give Him my stained clothes, and He gives me new garments, clean and white. This is love. When we have experienced the depth of this love for us, we know we can face anything because God's love covers us. His love moves us to perseverance. His love moves us to find rest in who He is. And His love helps me find out who I really am so I can get up, and in Him live a life that pleases the Father.

Read: John 8:2-11.

Reflect: This woman was caught in the act of adultery, but Jesus approached her anyway. He got down to her level, looked her in the eyes, and said, "I do not condemn you." One encounter with Him is all it takes to experience God's redemption. How have I seen God's love in my life? Have I been redeemed? Do I truly believe that God loves me?

Pray: *Dear God, thank You for Your love. Thank You for thinking that I am worth dying for. Help me to experience Your love every day and to live like I am redeemed and loved by You. Amen.*

DAY 20

Two major themes through this book are perspective and identity. Both of these have so much to do with the way our lives are steered. Author Lysa TerKeurst says, "We will steer where we stare." Wherever our focus is, that is where we will end up, so it is important for us to be aware of where we are staring. Are we focusing on disappointment and failure? Are we focusing on doubt and fear? Are we focusing on worry? Take a minute and do a heart-check. Where is your focus right now?

Today, let's shift our gaze to Christ. When our eyes are locked with His, we can see what He sees. We get a glimpse into His heart, and that is enough. It is enough to shift our perspective, and it is enough for us to see our true identity. On this side of eternity, it is impossible to lock eyes with Him without His help, and that is why it is vital to stay close to Him. To draw near. To walk with Him… and even more, abide in Him.

John 1 says that the Word became flesh and made His *dwelling* among us. In the literal translation, this means that He came and *tabernacled* among us; He lived among us. He made His home among us. Because He did this, we can now dwell, abide, and *tabernacle* in Him. He is our home. We are found *in* Him.

Colossians 3:3 (NIV) says, "For you died, and your life is now hidden with Christ in God." When we give our lives to Jesus, we are surrendering completely. It's a total abandonment of our own dreams, our aspirations, what we think is best for us and we let God take over. This might sound extreme and weird, but it's actually quite beautiful. It's not a surrender based on fear, or an abandonment based on blind loyalty to an obsessive being who wants domineering control of me—it's based on love. When you love someone, you come together and it's no longer *my* life but *our* life. I love Jesus so much because of who He is and all He's done for me, that my response is giving myself completely to Him because I love Him. My life is no longer my own in the best sense possible. I share it with the Lover of my soul, my life is His and in Him, I'm learning so much more about myself than I could ever on my own.

If you want to find out who you really are, you have to search *through* Christ because your life is *hidden* in Him. If you want to find out more about you, you have to find out more about Him. It's a beautiful relationship. It's one that grows deeper and deeper the closer you get. And the closer you get, the more clearly you can hear and see.

Here are just a few things God has to say about you: You are *loved*. You are *enough*. You are *chosen*. You are *forgiven*. You are *free*. You are *victorious*. You are *whole*. You are *unique*. You are *inspiring*. You are *redeemed*. You are *worth it*. You are *His*.

Read: Psalm 139:1-18 and Ephesians 3:14-19.

Reflect: Jesus, You surrendered it all for me, now lead me to surrender my all for You.

Pray: *Dear God, thank You because I am fearfully and wonderfully made. Help me to fully grasp just how great Your love is for me. Amen.*

DAY 21

Can you hear God's voice when He speaks to you? Not a literal voice, but the stirring of your heart in response to something He has opened your eyes to see. Perhaps God is nudging you to forgive someone. To do something that you don't want to do but know is right. To send a card to a hurting friend. To take a bowl of soup to a neighbor who's sick.

God speaks in many ways. Can you hear Him? It's okay if you struggle to hear His voice. There are so many examples of people in the Bible who struggled to identify and hear God's voice. As a child Samuel heard God speak, but he didn't know it was God, and it took him a while to realize it. But once he did, he opened up his heart to listen. Moses heard God through a bush that was on fire but didn't burn. In his conversation with God, he was listening, but not really hearing the message because it was being clouded by his own doubt and insecurities. But through the conversation God kept insisting that God Himself was enough for what Moses needed to do.

In the beginning, God created the heavens and the earth, and it was good. He made mankind, and it was good. He made us to be in communion with Him, and it was good. He came and walked in the garden together with Adam and Eve, and it was good. God's voice was clear to them, and all was good. However, when the serpent came and added his voice into the mix, Eve had a choice. She chose to quiet God's voice and allow the serpent's voice to become louder. She began to doubt God and, in effect, her own identity in her Creator.

One of the most amazing promises in the Bible is that you are His. You belong to the King of heaven. You are no longer some foreigner or stranger... you are His son, His daughter. God Himself is enough for you. And because of that, there is a room waiting for you in His heavenly home. There is a seat with your name on it at His table. You are His. Take a minute and let that soak in. The Creator of the universe, who spoke our entire universe into motion, loves you and wants to speak to you. Are you listening? We are nothing but a speck in the light of the galaxies, yet we matter enough that God's Son would choose to leave His throne and glory to become like us, walk among us, and die for us so that we could live eternally with Him. You are His. He loves you.

Listen to His voice. Listen to the voice that says you are a part of His family, that you are adopted into a new covenant of love sealed by Christ's blood. Listen to the voice that tells you that He will never leave you. His voice is enough. I invite you to read today's verses and sit with God; let yourself be a little uncomfortable with silence, and just hear what He has to say to you.

Read: Romans 8:14-17 and Jeremiah 31:3.

Reflect: How does knowing my identity in Christ help me to hear His voice? Am I willing to listen and obey?

Pray: *Dear God, help me to never forget that I am Yours. Please speak to me and guide me through Your Word, Your Spirit, and fellow believers. Amen.*

DAY 22

IN THE DEEPEST STORMS OF MY LIFE, THE LAST THING I thought of doing was jumping for joy. The amount of grief and loss I felt at certain times in my life were so insurmountable that all I could do was focus on the reality that was in front of me. I remember when I was a first-grade teacher, I had just brought my kids to lunch and was in my classroom getting some things ready for the next period. My phone was blowing up with messages from our prayer chain group text. I start scrolling and my heart sank inside of me when I read the words, "Please pray for Pastor Silvio. He is going to the emergency room because they found something in his head." I dropped my phone and forgot how to breathe. At that moment one of my colleagues walked in and saw me mid-panic attack and came to help me. Pastor Silvio is my dad. I had received the news that my dad was going to the ER because they found something in his head. He had been suffering through heavy migraines for many months leading to that moment, so my head jumped to the worst conclusions.

Friends, anxiety is real. Panic is real. Feeling a loss of control for the situations thrown at you is real. But what is also real is the presence of Jesus through it all. My colleague who God placed there at the right time, hugged me, and reminded me of my faith that was being clouded by the bad news I had just received. She helped to take my focus and bring it back *home*—back to Jesus. It took a long minute, but I got there. And for the days and months after that I had to continue to make the conscious decision to shift my perspective from doubt to faith.

Paul's message to the churches always included something to this nature as well. In Philippians 4, he encourages believers to *rejoice.* Interesting word. Rejoicing is easy when things are going well, but not so easy when times are tough. However, Paul tells them to rejoice, and then again, rejoice! Why should we rejoice? Because we know that the Lord is near. We know that He is closer than our breath. We know that we can cast all our anxieties and cares on Him because He loves us.

As we choose to rejoice, we are choosing *surrender.* As we surrender, an exchange begins to take place: all of us for all of Him. We choose to lay everything down, so that all of Him can come alive in us. This brings us His peace—the kind of peace that goes way beyond what we can explain or imagine. The kind of peace that we can have in the middle of a storm. This peace shifts our gaze to heaven, where we can fix our mind on things above—where we are actively trading our thoughts of fear, anxiety, worry, and doubt for whatever is right, pure, noble, and true. I wasn't rejoicing because my dad had a serious health scare. I rejoiced because I had confidence that God was with me, and in the process, I gave Him my panic and He gave me His peace.

This level of surrender takes a lifetime to develop. We're being refined day by day. It's okay not to have it all together. I don't have it all together. Just know that it's better to struggle *in Christ* than apart from Him.

Read: Philippians 4:4-8.

Reflect: What shifts can I make in my life to help me transition from a place of fear to a place of surrender and thinking of *things above*?

Pray: *Dear God, I surrender all that I have and all that I am to You. If I have You, I have everything. Amen.*

DAY 23

WE WERE MADE TO WORSHIP. NOW, I KNOW THAT'S A churchy word… but to worship means to give yourself up in devotion, to honor, to make something the most important thing in your life. We were made to worship God, but in the brokenness of our world, there are many things that come to compete against Him, so we bow to other things instead, and not God, and this creates problems deep within our soul. We were made to worship God who gives us peace, assurance of His presence in our life, purpose, identity, strength, etc. All good things that help us to navigate with confidence when things go sideways. However, we bow down to other things—idols, if you will. We choose to bow down to money, making it the most important thing in our life. Or we choose to bow down to sex and hook-up culture confusing lust for love. The list can go on and on. Point is, you're bowing down to something. What is it?

There's a story in the book of Daniel in which three young men refused to bow to a king's gold idol. The king was furious and threatened to have them thrown into a hot furnace. Their continued refusal despite this threat enraged the king to the point where he commanded the furnace to be heated seven times hotter than normal before throwing them in. Because they went against what culture and society demanded, they got "burned." Sound familiar? Today it would sound like, "they got cancelled." They got thrown into the fiery furnace, but they didn't burn up. A fourth man, who looked like "a son of the gods" (Daniel 3:25, NIV) joined them and protected them!

I don't know about you, but sometimes it seems like someone out there is turning up the heat. The enemy knows he's been defeated, but he's still trying to take down as many as he can. How does he do this? By turning up the heat. The phrase "if you can't stand the heat, get out of the kitchen" doesn't apply here. As believers we are going to face the "heat" in this world, and while we could choose to run from it, don't! Why not?

The furnace is hot, but there's another in the fire, Jesus, who will be right there with you. As with the three men, He walks with you in the fire, and the flames will not harm you because there is One who is mightier and fiercer than any flame. We have been called to stand out, to be different, and to not conform to the patterns of this world. We've been set apart to bow before God, the Heavenly King. Although some days will be harder than others, our faith walk with Jesus is so worth it. It is worth everything. Don't give up. Keep pressing on. He will see you through. He is faithful. Stand your ground.

There is something we learn when we're in the fire: Jesus is present. As Christian singer/songwriter and author Sheila Walch says, "Peace is not the absence of trouble, but the presence of Christ." In the fire we learn what trust is. Can you say to the idols trying to get your attention,

"I will not bow down before you. God can save me from the fire, but even if He doesn't, I still won't bow down to anything but Him"? That is a firm declaration from a heart that knows in Whom it trusts.

Read: Daniel 3.

Reflect: What idols am I bowing down to? What can I do to activate a faith that perseveres through the fire?

Pray: *Dear God, thank You for the promise that You walk with me through life's challenging fires. Thank you that You are with me because I need You now more than ever. Amen.*

DAY 24

In October of 2018, I was preaching at a church anniversary event in Paraguay. We were in the pastor's car on the way to the church when it started to rain, and then…pour! Before we knew it, the roads were flooding, and the water was rising fast, even though we were going uphill. I remember being particularly afraid because there were no guardrails to keep us from sliding off the road and over the hill. Suddenly the pastor stopped the car, put on the emergency brake, and said, "Pray!" An enormous wave of water was heading straight towards us from the top of the hill. I was too scared to pray. I saw people being swept away by the fierce wave, and all I could think about was how that would be the day I died.

However, it was not my time. God met me in the middle of that literal storm and reminded me who *He* was. Once I remembered who *He* was, I was able to remember who *I* was in Him. I started to pray—the rain stopped, and against the waves and laws of physics, the car drove up the hill, and we got to the church safely. It doesn't make sense. I shouldn't be alive. Fear almost won that day, but faith prevailed. When we got to the church there was a group of people there waiting for us saying, "Are you okay? God told us to come here and pray for your lives."

Later that night, God took me to Isaiah 43 and reminded me of this treasure of promises:

Do not fear: God is with you. He fills you with courage. He is all around you. Be fearless.

I have redeemed you: You have been bought with His blood. You have been set apart. You are chosen. He loves you so very much. He thinks you're worth dying for.

I have summoned you by name: He calls you by name no matter where you are or what you've done. He gives you a new name and a new identity found in Him.

You are mine: You are His. There is nothing that can separate you from His love. Just soak it in. Live in Him every day.

The waters: When the waves get big and the storm begins to rage, don't forget they are still obedient to the sound of His voice. He is walking with you through the waters. Let the water cleanse and refresh you.

The fire: He is with you when you walk through the fire. There is no life challenge too hard or too difficult that God can't walk you through. Just hold on to Him. Let Him lead. Let the flames purify, restore, and refine you.

What the enemy meant for evil that day in Paraguay, God used for good. It wasn't the end of my story; it was a moment that redefined everything for me. Perhaps you've been in a similar situation where you can look back and say, "Wow, the hand of God was there!" But the truth is that you don't need a near-death experience to look back and see how God was there. He is always there. He is always with you. He works all things for good, even when it doesn't make sense.

Read: Isaiah 43:1-2 and Genesis 50:20.

Reflect: God loves me and will take care of me.

Pray: *Dear God, thank You for watching over me. Thank You for Your protection and the assurance that You are all I need. Amen.*

DAY 25

THE PROPHET ISAIAH DECLARED TO ISRAEL THAT THE LORD had anointed him to proclaim, "the year of the Lord's favor." They would receive comfort and the Lord's provision, "a crown of beauty instead of ashes, the oil of joy instead of mourning, and a garment of praise instead of a spirit of despair." What wonderful news that must have been!

We are now alive in Christ, not dead in our sins—"beauty for ashes." We can live with the hope that we will see more of such beauty-for-ashes exchanges in our lifetime because of who God is. But how does this happen? For there to be beauty and regrowth and rebirth, there must be some sort of destruction and death—ashes. For example, the leaves on a tree must die and fall to the ground before we can enjoy the beauty of new leaves in the spring.

Although the words of Isaiah were meant for ancient Israel, those promises are still alive and active for us today *if* we are putting our trust in the God of Israel. No matter what kind of year you may be having, you can believe that it is the year of the Lord's favor because Jesus is present. No matter what is happening around you, you can believe that you will see beauty for ashes because Jesus is at work.

No matter the sorrow you may be experiencing, you can grieve with hope because Jesus rose from the dead. Even if you feel like the very ground underneath your feet is shaking, you can be confident that Jesus is solid ground and that all ruins will be restored in Him. He turns wastelands into gardens. He springs up something new from the old. This is what He does because of who He is.

I remember driving on the highway, and to my right out of the passenger side window, I could see a huge fire consuming the land. At first glance it looked quite scary and wild. But as I kept driving, I saw that it was a controlled fire—they were clearing the land so they could work and build upon it. There were firefighters and field workers on the outskirts making sure that everything was contained. I felt God say, *the fires in your life that have seemed wild, scary and out of control—I was there. And though they didn't come from me, I used them to help clear the land of your heart and make something beautiful."*

It's okay if you don't see it now. Our perspective is quite limited, but know that He is at work. If you asked me to declare at certain moments of my life that it was the year of the Lord's favor, I would probably have looked at you with so much contempt in my heart because of how I felt like everything was falling apart for me. There are moments where all we see are the ashes—the ruins. But I promise, He's there too. Sometimes it's in the looking back and connecting all the dots where you can sit back and say, "Wow. You really were there." Something I like to remind my heart is that my life isn't falling apart, it's falling into place. Don't take my word for it, take His. The promise of His presence is one of the greatest of all time.

Dare to believe Him, even if you don't see it yet. He is making all things beautiful in His time.

Read: Isaiah 61.

Reflect: How have I seen the Lord's favor in my life this season?

Pray: *Lord, You know my heart. You know that there are times when I really struggle to see You. Help me remember that my trust, my confidence, and my joy does not depend on my personal situation. Because You are alive, I can believe that You can take the ashes in my life and make them beautiful. Amen.*

DAY 26

Have you ever prayed for something and felt like God just wasn't listening? Or have you felt so alone and wondered if God would ever show up? Maybe you have even told God, *"God, you're too late!"* Maybe you've even considered that He isn't real because you just can't seem to find Him. Well, you're not alone.

There are moments in life that shake the ground beneath our feet, and we feel like no matter where we look, we just can't find sense, reasoning, or logic. It's like we can't find God. This happened to Mary and Martha when their brother Lazarus was sick. They sent word to Jesus to come heal Lazarus because they knew they were close friends. They knew that if Jesus could heal random strangers, he would *surely* do it for them because they were *friends.*

However, to their dismay, Jesus didn't come. They watched their brother die. Can you put yourself in their shoes for a minute? *Where is Jesus? Will He ever come? Does He care? Can we trust Him anymore?* Well, Jesus appeared four days later—*four long days of grief*—but Martha's response is extraordinary. Apart from being real and raw with the Lord and saying, "Lord, if you had been here, my brother would not have died," she also acknowledged, "But I know that even now God will give you whatever you ask." This is the kind of faith that needs to be activated within us. The kind of faith that can look at your dead brother's body and *still* believe that God is God, and God is good. The kind of faith that is *still* willing to trust even when things didn't turn out our way.

Then Jesus does something surprising: He asks them to move the stone that was sealing Lazarus's tomb. This is where our perspective is challenged. Can I believe that someone is going to come out of the tomb after watching him die and be buried? Can I be obedient to move the stone that has been sealing in my own emotions, my disappointment, my fears, my addictions, my trauma? Jesus spoke out Lazarus's name after He wept. Yes, Jesus wept. He felt the sting of death because it was not meant for us, but He didn't keep weeping because He knew what was going to happen: He would conquer death. So, He called out to Lazarus, and Lazarus came out of the grave! Jesus was not late, and He wasn't denying or ignoring His friends. He just knew that the end of the story would bring God glory in a way that His friends could not understand at the time.

Jesus is calling out your name today. Will you come out of your tomb? Jesus is calling out to your situation today; it might not come out the way you expect, but where Jesus is, there is resurrection, restoration, and life. Believe and trust. You can live with the assurance of hope in the shadow of the cross and in the light of an empty tomb!

Read: John 11.

Reflect: I am the one the Lord loves. He's never late. He is always on time.

Pray: *Dear God, help me learn to have confidence in the fact that Your timing is perfect. It's hard to trust when I cannot see You, but I know You're there, and I know You are at work because that is Your promise to me. Amen.*

DAY 27

Sometimes it's hard to remember and speak the promises of God. It is in moments of despair—in moments of anxiety, worry, and doubt—that we forget to Whom we belong. It's in those precise moments, however, that we need to remind our soul *not to fear* because we are His. It's in these moments that we need to command ourselves to "bless the Lord, O my soul: and all that is within me, bless his holy name" (Psalm 103:1, NIV).

What does it take to move onward, especially in the midst of pain, suffering, and chaos? It is in our nature to want to press forward, but it is also in our nature to be frightened at the sight of the storm. Even so, Jesus comes, meets us where we are, and gives us all that we need to take steps of faith—even when we don't want to, even when we can't see what the next step is.

For Paul and Silas this was an incredibly difficult challenge because they were walking where God led them, preaching and teaching the Good News about Jesus near and far—and yet they ended up physically beaten and in prison. It's very hard to move around in a prison cell, particularly if your hands are chained and your feet shackled. But in that cell, they chose to sing songs and worship. God showed up and shook the ground in a violent earthquake that broke their shackles and opened the prison doors. This happened. For real.

Just because you can't see anything happening when you cry out to God doesn't mean that God has left you. Paul and Silas couldn't move their feet, but their lips weren't bound, and they let loose hymns of praise from the heart of their jail cell. It was a praise so genuine, so steadfast, that their chains were broken. Foundations were shaken. Prison doors swung open wide.

No matter what the situation is around you, no matter what is bound and chained, the only one that allows for your praise to be bound is you. It's not your situation. It's not injustice. It's not unrest. It's not the storm. These things definitely make us feel certain ways, but they only have the power over us that we give them. Praise is not a denial of what's around us; it's the acknowledgment of the God who is above it all.

In the moments of my deepest despair, God taught me that the only way out was through worship. He forged in me a faith that was refined as I chose to worship Him in the middle of pain and questioning. After time, instead of running to God as a last resort it has become my first response. It took a lot of time, and I'm not perfect at it, but I can confidently say that worship changed my life. So, I invite you to choose worship. Quiet all the noise around you and play worship music and let the words rest upon your soul until there's breakthrough. Don't give up. Singing and praying may not change the actual situations you're in, but they change the way you see them and respond to those situations. Choose worship, every time.

Read: Acts 16:16-34.

Reflect: Is worship my first response to chaos? If not, what steps can I take to shift my perspective so that I can praise and worship God?

Pray: *Dear God, it's easy to worship when everything is good. It gets harder when things do not go my way. It gets almost impossible when I feel like You've abandoned me. Help me remember this fundamental truth: You are always with me. Since that is true, I will always have a reason to praise. Amen.*

DAY 28

THERE IS A STORY IN THE BIBLE ABOUT A MAN NAMED Moses. Moses was born to a Hebrew woman but because of an infanticide he was rescued from, he grew up in Pharaoh's household as royalty. He had a lot of built-up anger that came out one day as he killed an Egyptian man who was hurting a Hebrew slave. He was very afraid after that incident and ran away. Moses spent years trying to make sense of his life, and just when things were settling down, God called him *by name* through the flames of a burning bush and told him to go back to Egypt and be the man to free his fellow Israelites from their captivity. Moses was like, "Come again, Lord? No. Nope. You're mistaken. I can't even talk right. I have a really bad st… st…st…stutter."

Moses was in the very presence of God, yet he made up every excuse in the book to prove to God why he wasn't qualified for the job. Thank goodness God doesn't see us the way we see ourselves. Moses finally trusted God, and God changed his story. God changed Moses from murderer to deliverer. Moses led his people out of Egypt, and they saw God's wonders and miracles as they stepped into freedom. Knowing Moses' murderous past, God still chose him and called him by name and chose him to free the Hebrews from captivity. If God can do that, there's nothing He can't do.

God wants to work in you and through you, for His glory. What excuses are you bringing to the table? For me, it was my divorce. I had voices telling me I could never be a pastor and never be able to lead worship again. I was told that ministry was no longer an option for me, and I believed it for a while. When I felt God calling me to seminary, I said, "I'm not qualified." "There are better people out there than me." "My past makes me not worthy to be used by God." Those were all half-truths. I'm not qualified—there are better people out there with lives way more put together than mine—I am not worthy—BUT GOD. My two favorite words put together. *But God* called me by name in spite of my short comings…and the rest is history. My past has no hold on me. I am not walking in shame, for I am covered by His grace. His grace rewrote my story.

What are you telling God about yourself to prove that you don't have what it takes? The beauty of the Lord is that He isn't interested in what you can't do but what *He* can do through you. All you need is an open heart, an open mind, and obedience. Once Moses said *yes*, it wasn't an easy road. Pharaoh opposed him and made the assignment very difficult; but in every step of the way, God showed up with signs and wonders proving that He would not leave Moses alone. When God is the One calling, He will come through. Don't be afraid. Let God rewrite your story.

Read: Exodus 3:1-12.

Reflect: God changed Moses' story. He wants to change mine. Have I allowed God to step in? If not, am I now willing to say yes to God's plans for me?

Pray: *Dear God, it's amazing to see how You can change someone's life and give them a whole new story. Teach me Your ways. Help me to believe everything You say about who I am in You. Amen.*

DAY 29

We were created to be in communion with God, Who is love (1 John 4:8, NIV). When we search near and far to be loved here on earth, we are also searching for God's eternal love. We were created to be loved because that was God's design from the beginning. When we don't know Jesus, we go to great lengths to try to fill this void that can only be satisfied through Him. When we don't feel seen, heard, and loved in a relationship, we begin to doubt the foundation of that relationship. We question whether the love and devotion are true. While relationships here on this side of eternity are fragile, the love that God has for you is unbreakable. There is nothing you can do to deserve it, and nothing you can do to escape it. He freely gives it to you.

In Genesis 16 and 21, we are introduced to Sarah, Abraham's wife, and her servant, Hagar. After many years, Sarah seemed unable to have children, even though God had promised them that they would have a son. Sarah then told Abraham to sleep with Hagar in order to help God fulfill His promise (because obviously God needed help, right?) Wrong. God didn't need their help. Hagar indeed had a son, Ishmael, but he wasn't the promised one. Hagar goes on to experience rejection and loneliness. Sarah, with Abraham's support, then sends Hagar and Ishmael to the desert. But God met Hagar right there—right in the middle of the desert. Right in the middle of her fears and doubts. He told her not to fear—He promised that He would make a great nation through her son, and He provided water for her in the desert.

My life was changed when God met me in my desert, and I felt Him like Hagar did. Everything changed when I discovered that He saw me and that He cared for me. It's easy to read these stories and ask a lot of questions. It's easy to go through life's storms and desert seasons and ask God a lot of questions, or even be tempted to do worse… not even bother. To go on believing that He's not real. Or living life believing that He's real, but just not interested in you. I want to encourage you today to open the eyes of your heart and find God. He's there. When you find Him, let Him speak. Even in the desert, He has a plan.

God sees you and hears you as He did Hagar. He isn't a distant God. He is closer than you think. Maybe you've felt like you deserve the desert you're walking through, and God couldn't care less about you. You're wrong. He loves you. He sees you. He hears you. Maybe you're in the desert and you have no idea how you got there, and you feel alone. You're not alone. God loves you. He sees you. He hears you. The desert times cannot stop His love for you, and your mistakes are not enough to stop the flow of His devotion to you. God is for you, now and forever.

Read: Genesis 16 and Genesis 21:1-19.

Reflect: God loves me. God sees me. God hears me.

Pray: *Dear God, thank You for seeing me, hearing me, and always loving me. Amen.*

DAY 30

IN ANCIENT TIMES, INFORMATION WAS PASSED DOWN FROM generation to generation through the oral tradition of storytelling. Families would gather together and listen to the elders tell the tales of the past. This is how the younger generations learned everything God did, from the glory of creation to the great exit from Egypt and beyond. They also learned that the Israelites bowed to other gods, which led to seven years of oppression by the Midianites and other foreign nations. They were at the mercy of an enemy people. But God didn't abandon His people. He met them right where they were and reminded them of who He was. How?

An angel appeared to a man named Gideon and called him "mighty warrior." This was ironic because Gideon was in a winepress, basically a cave—hiding out trying to avoid the enemy threshing wheat when this angel appeared and told him that he would deliver Israel from the enemy. *What?* Like Moses, who we talked about a few days ago, Gideon didn't believe God and asked for proof multiple times. When Gideon finally surrendered to the Lord and obeyed His calling, Gideon assembled an army of thirty thousand men. But God kept decreasing those numbers until there were only three hundred soldiers.

This would be the mighty army led by the mighty warrior that chose to trust in the Lord. Wild. This absolutely does not make sense.

But that's just it. God doesn't see us the way we see ourselves. He sees us through His eyes of purpose and destiny, and He promises to always be with us. God's plans are not ours. His reasoning is not ours. When He calls, it may sometimes sound absolutely ridiculous because we are so used to seeing things from our own perspective, aligned with our finite reality. We don't see ourselves as "mighty warriors" called by a powerful God. We don't have to understand or agree; we just have to trust and obey. Gideon won the victory for Israel with some trumpets, jars, and torches! I love the revelation that God gave me with this story to help me fight my own battles. Trumpets—praising even when the enemy army is near. Jars—remembering that I'm just a jar in His hands. I can easily break, but in His hands, I can do great things. Torches—it's all about His light in me. His light will guide the way. By worshiping, remembering that I am a jar in His hands and letting His light shine on my path, I can walk through anything.

No matter what you are facing, you can trust God. Clear your heart of desires that are not from the Holy Spirit. Remove all lies, doubts, and fears. Surrender to God as Gideon did, acknowledging that God's plans are greater than your plans. Total trust in God and abandonment to self is how we become mighty warriors and see victory. And in all things, remembering that it's not the victory that tastes the sweetest, it's the promise of the Presence of

God walking with us every single day of our lives. There is nothing better than that.

Read: Judges 6:11-17 and Judges 7.

Reflect: It is time to come out of hiding. God has plans and purposes for me that are beyond what I could ever think, ask, or imagine.

Pray: *Dear God, thank You for seeing the mighty warrior in me. Help me to trust and obey, especially when Your assignment for my life doesn't make sense to me. Help me to remember that You are in control, and You've never lost a battle. Amen.*

DAY 31

Growing up in New Jersey, I could see the seasons change from my window. Fresh snow covered the ground in the winter, little buds began to decorate the trees in the spring, luscious green leaves and grass colored the summer landscape, and then autumn broke through with breathtaking arrays of reds, oranges, and yellows. The thing about seasons is that they are always transitioning. No season lasts forever.

The same is true about the seasons of life. In what may seem to be a spiritual winter—cold, barren, and desolate—God is working unseen, preparing for the springtime. Your season is coming. Hang tight. What you see as a wasteland, God sees as a garden ready to bloom. What you see as an end, God sees as a beginning. What you see as ashes, God sees as beauty.

The Lord is faithful. He will water the seed He planted until it's time to harvest. Keep yourself close to His streams of living water. They are what will keep you from running dry in the drought. His fountain never runs dry. Your season is coming. It is the time of fulfillment. The time of restoration of dreams. The time of renewal of vision. Don't give up. Your season is coming. There's a line in a song by Hillsong that says, *"For His promise is loyal, from seed to sequoia."* He will complete what He started in you.

If you plant a seed and you want it to grow, you have to take care of it. You have to make sure it gets enough sunlight, enough water. You have to make sure the atmosphere is just right so that little seed can grow into what it's supposed to be. God planted His seed in us, but it doesn't just stop there. There's work to be done. Surrender, trust, obedience, and faith all need to be activated in us to help us grow into what God intends us to be—trees of righteousness!

These trees of righteousness are not like the trees you can see from your window. These trees have very special properties. Their leaves do not fear the heat; their fruit never fails; their leaves never wither; they always prosper. Why? Because they are planted next to "streams of water," the One and only source of life: Jesus. Life by God's stream isn't always without risk, but the water keeps you alive and well through any and every season. You are a beautiful seed called to be a great tree of righteousness that will bring nourishment and shade to many. Stay by the water.

Read: Psalm 1, Jeremiah 17:7-8, and Ezekiel 47:12.

Reflect: What season am I in? How has God shown His faithfulness in this season?

Pray: *Dear God, thank You for being with me in every season. You are all-knowing and all-powerful, and I can rest assured by Your streams of nourishing water, knowing that in You I will blossom and flourish. Teach me to trust in Your timing in each season. Amen.*

DAY 32

Raise your hand if you worry. Yeah, I know. I'd raise both my hands and feet! We have bills to pay. Debts to pay off. Jobs to keep. Food to eat. Clothes to wear. School to get through. Relationships to nurture. The list goes on and on. However, through it all, Jesus tells us to trust Him, to trust that He is our Provider.

Worried about money? All gold and silver belong to the Lord. Worried about the future? He says His plans for you are good. Worried that nothing makes sense? He says that His ways are higher than ours. Worried that God has no clue what He's doing? He works all things for our good.

Don't worry. Trust. It's easier said than done. However, I've learned that as we practice trust, our reaction time to God's instructions become shorter and shorter. Let me explain. When I get into my crazy worry mode, the amount of time I spend in that mode becomes less and less as I learn to trust Him. I get into panic mode, but then my trust mode begins to kick in, and I begin to worship and allow God to comfort my heart. Some days are better than others. We're human; we're going to worry—but we don't need to stay there. We have a God who can handle it all. If He spoke the universe into existence, He can take care of every single one of my needs.

One night I was praying and asking God to help me trust and to give me a way out of a difficult situation I was going through. The Lord whispered to me, "Close your eyes." As I closed my eyes, I could see myself standing on a flat rock suspended in midair. He told me to take a step. There was nothing to step on, but I began to move my foot anyway. As my foot was ready to land on nothing, a steppingstone appeared. I looked down at the stone, and it was engraved with promises in Scripture: *I will never leave you nor forsake you. I will finish what I started in You. I am your Shepherd. You will lack nothing. I am raising a banner for you.* When I opened my eyes, I realized that I didn't need to know the way out. All I needed to know in my situation was that He was there with me. He would make a way.

Surrender your worry to the Lord. Close your eyes and watch Him make a way.

Read: Matthew 6:25-34.

Reflect: What are some things I am worrying about? I surrender them to God. I believe that He will provide a steppingstone and make a way for me.

Pray: *Dear God, I know that You are with me, You will never leave me, and You will take care of me. Help me to abandon all outcomes to You and know that You will provide the steppingstones that I need exactly when I need them. Amen.*

DAY 33

MANY DIFFERENT KINDS OF WINDS BLOW THROUGH OUR lives, and it's easy to trust them when they are favorable and blowing in the direction we want. But winds can change at any moment, and what was in your favor at one moment can blow violently against you the next. Your trust should be only in the Lord your God, Who is unaffected by the changes. He will keep you steady through them.

The ship that Paul was traveling in got caught in a hurricane on his way to defend his actions before Caesar. For three days, the winds and waves were against them, and the people on board lost all hope of rescue and survival. However, in the midst of the storm, Paul stood up and encouraged all those on board because an angel of the Lord had come to him and told him: Take courage. You will lose the ship, but you will go to Caesar, and everyone will live. Believe God because He said so.

We can find courage in the middle of the storm because we know Whose we are and Whom we serve. We need to be ready to experience loss because it's inevitable. After the crew threw most of their supplies overboard, Paul told them that they would lose the ship, too. There will be times when we will suffer tremendous loss in the storm. But our trust in God can propel us beyond what we can physically see. Our trust helps us to know that the greatest loss here on earth cannot compare to the greatest gain we have in Jesus.

I mentioned in an earlier devotion that I was praying for my struggling marriage. Unfortunately, the winds shifted for us. Separation and divorce were one of the hardest storms I've been through. However, that's where I truly began to understand that a life in Christ doesn't mean *no* loss. It doesn't mean *no* sorrow. It doesn't mean *no* death. It means that if our life is anchored in Jesus, then we are going to be okay. It might not make sense, but in the end, it's going to be okay. The storm affected me, but it didn't define me. God brought hope to an incredibly hopeless situation and met me right where I was.

Genuine hope and confidence are often forged by the storms of this world, but a great reward awaits those who persevere until the end; to those who make Jesus their hope. Don't put your hope in the favorable winds or in your ship. Don't fear the shifting of winds. Don't fear the shipwreck. God is still good, and He is still in control.

Read: Acts 27:13-44.

Reflect: Where does my hope lie? Am I easily blown away by the changing winds of this life?

Pray: *Dear God, thank You for being constant. Thank You for the eternal hope that pushes past the temporary storms of this life. Keep me centered on You, now and forever. Amen.*

DAY 34

Two of my favorite quotes are: "It's not over 'til it's over" and "God gives us grace for our race." We all have a track we are running on, and each one looks different. And sure, someone else's track might look more appealing than ours at times, but don't forget this truth: God gives *us* grace for *our* race. He is with us and will help us run our race with perseverance until the very end.

That's the key: perseverance. Don't stop. Don't quit. Keep pressing on. Jesus endured the cross. He will help you overcome. Just keep your eyes fixed on Him. Even if all seems lost and hopeless, even if you feel like you just can't do it anymore, keep pressing on. Your reward is waiting for you at the finish line. It's not a trophy you can hold. It's not a medal you can shine. It is a Crown of Life that is waiting for you as Jesus looks at you and says, "Well done, good and faithful one." The race will get hard, but it's so worth it.

By now, you already know that you have everything you need in Jesus. He gives you peace for the race because of who He is: the Prince of Peace. He promises to give you His peace at all times and in every way. He can do this for you because He is the Well that never runs dry.

All you need to do is drink from the Well and stay close to the Source.

The world awaited its Messiah—its Savior and Deliverer. The prophecy about Him was that He would be everything we could ever need. This prophecy wasn't just for Israel waiting for captivity to end; it extends to us today. We are found in this timeline where grace and mercy collide. To us, He is our Wonderful Counselor, and the truest comfort and hope lie in Him. He is our Mighty God, and nothing is impossible for Him. He is our Everlasting Father—*Abba*—who cares for us from now until forevermore. He is our Prince of Peace, and His very presence is enough to calm the storm within and around us. Dwell on how God has given you what you needed. If He's done it before, you can trust that He'll do it again.

Read: 2 Thessalonians 3:16 and Isaiah 9:1-7.

Reflect: How have I experienced God's grace in my race?

Pray: *Dear God, thank You for being with me in my race through life. I know that with You at my side, I can faithfully run the race and cross the finish line to claim the crown of eternal life. Amen.*

DAY 35

A MAJOR THEME THROUGHOUT OUR FORTY DAYS OF devotions together has been trust. Trusting in God. Abandoning all outcomes to God. Trusting and believing that God is good, and that He's good at being God—a phrase a pastor taught me. I may think I know what's best, and I'd really like to twist God's arm sometimes to get Him to play the role that I give Him in my script for my life. Sometimes I really wish that He'd just say the lines I've written for Him. The truth is … God knows better. He's the director. I need to remember my place. To some this may seem harsh—like He's the dictator and we're the subordinates. But it's quite the opposite. It's a beautiful dance of surrender—a true expression of intimacy and love. Allowing God to take the lead, as I follow and trust His move.

Trusting in the Lord means letting go. Think about this. When you're holding onto something, your hands are in a closed position. They are not open to receive what God wants to give you. Stop focusing on the getting (getting what *you* want, getting what you think you *need*, getting what you believe is *rightfully yours*). Let go. Open your hands and rest in God. Trust that He will provide. Trust that He will come through. I know that He's never failed me yet, and He won't start now. Trust Him with all your heart; He will make your path straight.

Ask God today to clear the clutter of your heart, everything and anything that is in the way of allowing you to fully trust in Him. Trust comes from letting God sit on the throne of your heart. If there are things fighting for that throne, then little by little your trust is going to sway towards whatever is currently seated there. Invite the Holy Spirit to do a deep clean, to strengthen your faith and renew your trust in Him. I invite you to sit for awhile and actually open up your hands as you ask God to help you let go of the things you weren't made to hold onto.

Read: Proverbs 3:5-6 and Isaiah 26:4.

Reflect: What are some things in my life that I still need to just "let go and let God"?

Pray: *Dear God, my ways seem so much better to me sometimes, but I know they're not. You always know exactly what I need, and You're so, so good to me. Teach me to trust You more with my whole heart. Clean out the clutter and sit on the throne of my heart. Amen.*

DAY 36

BLESSINGS FOLLOW OBEDIENCE. THAT'S THE WAY THE kingdom works. When you are seeking God, all of His goodness and blessings follow. However, when you are seeking the blessings, your focus is in the wrong place and you will never catch them. Seeking God's blessings instead of seeking Him is a tiresome chase that only leads to emptiness and burnout. Our allegiance should not be to what we can *get* from following God, but to God and God alone. And in reality, my pursuit of God is really my response to Him pursuing me first.

Look at Noah. He faithfully built the ark for what historians believe to have been seventy to a hundred and twenty years. He endured ridicule and mocking in the driest season ever, but when the flood came, he and his family were saved. Look at Moses. It took him a minute to finally surrender, but God used him to liberate a whole nation. Look at Abraham. God told him to move, and he did. God told him to wait for the son of the promise, and 25 years later he came. Blessings follow obedience. It's worth it to wait on God.

What's so frustrating about obedience is that we have to willingly surrender. We have to be okay with not being in control. We have to be okay with saying, "Okay God.

You've got this." It's not easy. But it's so worth it, and the blessings that follow are incredible. Don't forget this though: we don't serve God for what He can give us. We serve Him and love Him for *Who He is.* For what Christ did on the cross for us. We hold tight to His promises, but more than that, we cling to the Promise Giver. Don't cling to God for His *presents.* Stay close to him for His *presence.*

Read: Deuteronomy 28:1-14 and Matthew 6:33.

Reflect: How have I seen God's blessings in my life because of obedience? What are some areas I need to work on?

Pray: *Dear God, thank You for Your many blessings! I believe that incredible blessings are still to come. Help me to desire You more than Your blessings. Thank You for being so good to me. Amen.*

DAY 37

RESTING IN GOD'S PROMISES IS NOT EASY. AS TIME PASSES, it's easy to conform to the patterns of this world more and more, and the promises of God get lost in the background. His values get buried. His Word becomes less "relevant." For all these reasons and more, we need to stand true to who we are in Him and avoid swaying to the right or to the left, regardless of the shifts that society and culture make around us.

Caleb and Joshua, who were two of the twelve spies sent into Canaan to scope out the Promised Land, faced a difficult situation. They were so close to the land that God promised, ready to take it, but ten out of the twelve spies came back with a negative report: The people are very tall and much stronger than we are. We can't attack them and win!

The funny thing is that they weren't wrong, but they also weren't right, and that is how the enemy plays us into fear. The people were in fact bigger and stronger than the Israelites were, but if God said this was the Promised Land, then who was to say that they couldn't conquer it? The enemy shifts our perspective by entangling us in half-truths that makes us believe they are full truths. We need to shift the way we see these oncoming attacks and recognize them as half-truths (which make them lies) that are irrelevant in the light of God's promises—His truth.

Caleb and Joshua weren't falling for the deception, and they boldly stood up and said that if God promised, then He would deliver. It was not the popular opinion. In fact, no one listened to them, and the consequence was to wander for forty years in the wilderness—all for being stubborn, stiff-necked, hard-hearted, and unbelieving.

It's hard to assimilate that this happened to people who saw God's signs and wonders unveiled before their eyes. But it also proves the frailty of our hearts. Let us not forget the wonders of our God. Let us not be distraught by what we see. Instead, let us learn to trust solely on the words that come from God through the person of Jesus.

Though Caleb and Joshua walked in the desert for forty years, they received the reward that no one else did. They were able to set foot in the Promised Land when the time came because they had a *different spirit* than everyone else around them. Even if you don't see the benefits of your obedience now, don't worry—you will.

Read: Numbers 13 and Numbers 14:1-9.

Reflect: How do I see the world in front of me? Can I still believe God's promises even when everyone else tells me not to believe?

Pray: *Dear God, help me to trust Your promises and to stay faithful. Create in me an obedience that pushes past the things that seem much bigger and stronger than I am and help me to trust You. Amen.*

DAY 38

HAVE YOU EVER POURED OUT YOUR HEART BEFORE THE Lord and felt like He just wasn't paying attention? As if all your efforts were to no avail? *God seems to be listening to everyone but me.* Has this thought ever crossed your mind?

There's a woman in the Bible named Hannah, who had the same problem. All she ever wanted in life was to be a mom, and it just wasn't happening. She prayed and prayed and prayed some more; she prayed so much, with such passion and total abandon, that people thought she was drunk. But she wasn't. She was just in a place of pure desperation. Her prayers were flowing from a place of sadness, yet trust. She wasn't receiving her answer, yet she remained faithfully praying in the house of God.

We tend to give up after we don't see any movement up in the heavens in our favor. When things don't go our way, we blame God. But Hannah knew that the only place she could find what she was looking for was right there, on her knees in the house of the Lord. Through her disappointment month after month, year after year, she pressed on until ... the Lord granted her the desire of her heart!

All of our stories are different. Hannah got her miracle. You might receive what you're praying for, or you might not. God's answers can be "yes," "no," or "wait." Whatever God's answer is for you, keep pressing on. Keep trusting; God knows what He's doing. Remember that the enemy wants to make you doubt the goodness of God, but when you purposefully choose to remain in the center of His goodness, situations can come to shake you, but you will remain unmovable.

How do you remain in the center of His goodness? By praying without ceasing, like Hannah. Choose to be in a prayerful posture all day, every day. This doesn't mean you're going to become a monk and isolate yourself forever; it just means that your heart is ready to talk to God at any moment, and you're always ready to hear from Him. Choose joy and give thanks at all times. Yes, *all* times, because no matter what is happening around you, Jesus is good. There's always a reason to give thanks, even in moments where you might feel like He is silent. He's there. Can you push through the awkward silence? Can you keep pushing through when the awkward silence becomes untenably loud? Can you choose trust even when you don't feel Him? No matter where you're at right now, God is calling out to you. So lean in. Silence doesn't last forever.

Read: 1 Samuel 1:1-20 and 1 Thessalonians 5:16-18.

Reflect: How do I respond when God seems silent?

Pray: *Dear God, it's so hard to hear a "no" from You, but it's definitely harder to hear nothing. Teach me to always cling to You no matter what. Be my joy and my peace in seasons of waiting. Amen.*

DAY 39

We serve a faithful God, a God who is true to His word. If He said it, it will be done.

- Do you believe that He is faithful?
- Do you believe that He loves you?
- Do you believe that His plans for you are good?
- Do you believe that you are an overcomer?
- Do you believe that He will finish what He started in you?
- Do you believe that your whole family can be saved?
- Do you believe that you can weather any storm?
- Do you believe that life's challenges are winds and waves trying to keep you from trusting in Him?

You are everything He says you are. Let that sink in today. There is no wave too high and no wind too strong to derail God's plan for your life. Stay the course. Stay faithful. Stay connected to Him. Keep your eyes on Jesus in the midst of the storm. He will see you through. Stand up in faith and proclaim and believe all His promises to be true. It's time to take ownership of God's promises for you and believe them with all your heart.

It's easy not to trust because of the situations that come

our way. It's easy to question the goodness of God when bad things happen. From the beginning of time, it has been the enemy's strategy to get humanity to doubt God's good intentions and good will for creation. This is why the Bible is full of passages urging us and encouraging us to keep the faith. To keep trusting and believing in His goodness.

Trust that He is good even when you can't see it. Trust that He is good even if your marriage is falling apart. Trust that He is good even as sickness creeps its way through your door. Trust that He is good even if war breaks out around you. Trust that He is good even if things seem ridiculously unfair. Trust in God and continue to serve Him here on earth until you go home to be with Him, or until He comes again. That's what it's all about. Keep the faith dear friend, keep the faith.

Read: James 1:2-18 and 2 Corinthians 1:18-20.

Reflect: Do I believe that all of God's promises for my life are true?

Pray: *Dear God, thank You for promising to walk with me always. That's the greatest promise of all. Help me persevere; help me stay my course. I believe that You are with me in the winds and the waves, and that You are greater and more powerful. I will keep my focus on You and trust in You. Amen.*

DAY 40

I PRAY THAT YOU'VE HAD AN INCREDIBLE ENCOUNTER with the Lord throughout these past forty days. I pray that you've seen Jesus in a brand-new way. I pray that you can see a storm coming and know in your heart that God is still in control. Do not be afraid. Jesus is with you. The same God that's been revealing Himself to you during these devotions will be with you every single moment of every single day. You have one very important job to do: keep your eyes and heart focused on Him.

I pray that you have experienced healing, wholeness, love, and joy as you have trusted Him throughout these forty days. I also pray that you are aware that the enemy wants to take those things away as soon as he can because he does not want you to keep experiencing God's blessings. It might seem like a huge storm is against you after some smooth sailing—but fear not.

On day 1 we read in Mark 4 about how Jesus calmed the wind and the waves. Matthew 14 also tells a similar story. In both accounts Jesus told his disciples after they started becoming afraid of the fierce storm: "Take courage. It is I. Do not be afraid" (Matthew 14:27, NIV). Wind and waves will come in our lives, but they must still be obedient to Him. Take courage. There is no wave that Jesus can't overcome and no wind that He can't calm. He is powerful, and He is with you. As counterintuitive as this sounds—find comfort in the storm, because you know Jesus is near.

Peter saw Jesus, and he believed that if Jesus was walking on the water, so could he. So, he got out of the boat and actually *did* walk on water—until he broke eye-contact with Jesus to the waves. Then he began to sink. He cried out to Jesus for help, and Jesus immediately picked Peter back up and brought him to safety because that's the love He has for us.

As tempting as it may be to look at the wind and waves that are crashing around you, don't do it. Keep your eyes on Jesus. The storm will pass. But if you do look away, don't worry. Don't be afraid. Don't be ashamed. Just call out to Jesus, and He will pick you back up. Keep walking. Keep believing. Let every cell of your body believe in the goodness of God. Let every fiber of your being believe that the wind and the waves *still* know His name.

So today I want to make an invitation. If you have been navigating life without Jesus and you're in a boat and it's scary, but you see Jesus on the waters and you are hearing His call to you saying, "Come," then I invite you to pray and make Him the Lord and Savior of your life. Don't worry about what to say. It doesn't have to be fancy. Just pour out your heart and answer the call. If you've already given your life to Christ, but you feel like you're the Peter who's broken eye-contact with Jesus and now you're sinking and you need to be rescued, just call out. He is reaching out for you. Come home, child. He is waiting ever so lovingly for you.

Read: Matthew 14:22-33.

Reflect: How am I like Peter? How can I prepare my heart for the wind and waves that will come?

Pray: *Dear God, thank You for Your promises. I believe that no matter what I go through, You promise to be with me. Help me not to fear the storm, but to have the confidence that it must still be obedient to Your voice. Guide me in times of uncertainty and lead me in moments of weakness and fear. Fill me with Your courage, peace, and joy. Thank You, Lord! Amen.*

DAY 41

Okay. I couldn't let you leave without going into more depth on one of my favorite stories that we talked about during our 40 days together. It's more of a sandwich of stories, so hang tight. In Mark chapter 5 we see a man named Jairus approach Jesus because his daughter is dying. Jesus, being the interruptible guy He is, went with Him. On their way, Jesus gets interrupted again. A woman, unnamed, but labeled by her condition—hemorrhaging for 12 years, touches Jesus. She thought to herself, *I need to get to this man… if He healed others, I know He can heal me.*

But wait… she was a woman, and she was bleeding. Two big things that kept her isolated from community because she was considered unclean. Can you imagine her dilemma? Completely marginalized and outcast. No one wanted her around. She was labeled by her condition. Have you ever felt that way? I sure have. And the Bible goes on to explain that she spent all her money on different doctors trying to get better. Don't we do that too? If something is hurting, we go get it checked out. If it's really bad, we go for a second opinion. We do this with our souls too. We visit "soul doctors" if you will. We are too stressed out, so we go to Dr. Alcohol to numb the pain. We want to feel validation and pleasure, so we go to Dr. Hook-Ups and Dr. One-Night Stands. We hate the way we look so we go to Dr. Comparison, Dr. Excessive Workout or Dr. Food Disorder. We spend all we have on all the wrong doctors, when the only one that can heal us from the inside out is Jesus.

Well, this woman made that choice, and against all odds she went from behind and touched the edge of Jesus' cloak. She pushed through the crowd that was there, and Jesus felt power leave Him and she was immediately healed. To her dismay, Jesus called out, "who touched me?" *I've been caught. Now He will punish me.* She thought. But Jesus didn't call her out to shame her, but to name her. *Daughter, your faith has healed you.* It is the first and only time in the New Testament that Jesus uses the word *Daughter* referring to it as a name—as a proper noun. The nameless woman, labeled by her condition was given a name that day, all because of Jesus.

However, let's not forget that Jairus was still there. Can you imagine how He must've felt? *Good for you lady, but Jesus, I came to you first. What about me? Did you forget about my daughter?* Well, after this woman's miracle, Jairus got some news. His daughter had died. But Jesus, ignoring that news, looked at Jairus in the eyes and said, *don't be afraid, keep believing.* They kept going on their way until reaching Jairus' house, which was filled with professional criers, mourning the loss of the little girl who was 12 years old. Jesus told them to get out. The enemy sends his band of professional noise makers to keep you from hearing His truth. Kick them out. Don't be afraid. Keep believing. Then breaking even more social norms, Jesus walked into the dead girl's room, and more than that, He took the dead girl's hand and brought her back to life. He proved His power over disease and now death! There is nothing impossible for Him.

Now, look at these two stories side by side: Jairus had 12 years of a beautiful life with his daughter. The woman had 12 years of agony. Jairus was an important man. This woman was no one… she did not even have a name. Jairus was probably wealthy because he was an important man. This woman spent all she had leaving her with nothing. Jairus came publicly. The woman came in secret. They both thought they needed a physical touch. Jesus responded to Jairus with "delay." Jesus responded to the woman immediately. Jairus came publicly and his daughter was healed secretly. The woman came secretly and was healed publicly. These two people couldn't be more different, but what brought them together was their desperate need for Jesus. That's what links us to this story too.

So, whoever you are, wherever you are, Jesus loves you. He wants to give you a name. He wants to give you a new life. Don't let this journey end here. He gave His life for you on a cross, and by His own power, came back to life. This is really good news. Come to Him, and then share this good news with your friends. Understanding His story helps us to realize that His whole mission was us—to restore us to community, just as He did with this woman, and with Jairus' daughter. In restoring us to community, our faith is strengthened, and we can lean on each other as different storms of life come.

Read: Mark 5:21-42.

Reflect: How am I like Jairus? How am I like the woman? What noises in my life do I need to kick out so I can stop being afraid and keep believing?

Prayer: *Dear Jesus, thank You for being interruptible. Thank You for meeting me where I'm at and for calling me out not to shame me, but to name me and give me new life. Help me share this good news with others. Amen.*